Ventnor, Isle of Wight

The English Mediterranean

Michael Freeman

Ventnor and District Local History Society
Headquarters: Ventnor Heritage Museum, 11, Spring Hill, Ventnor PO38 1PE
www. ventnorheritage.org.uk

Ventnor, Isle of Wight: the English Mediterranean

List of Contents

A view of the Undercliff west of Ventnor, photographed early last century

Preface

This book is intended primarily as an historical guide for visitors and residents. It is a blend of conventional guide-book and local history, for it starts from the scene that meets the visitor's eye today and then seeks to unravel the story behind it. New visitors are often amazed that a town the size of Ventnor ever came to be built on so precipitous a coastal site. They are surprised by its diminutive beach (more a cove, which is what it was once called) and by the elaborate ranks of tall Victorian shopfronts that line its two main thoroughfares. It does not at all accord with the pattern of a conventional nineteenth-century seaside town, even though it started to become one in the decades that followed the arrival of the railway in 1866. The central clue to the town's development is to be found in its origin as a winter sanatorium, as a watering place that became celebrated for the equability of its winter climate, part of the famed Undercliff. From 1830, in particular, it became a prized resort for invalids, especially those afflicted with diseases of the chest. It became patronized by the rich and the famous, including British and foreign royalty, along with an ever-growing array of German and American citizens who were so seduced by its Mediterranean-like winters that they came back year after year. The inexorable outcome was an astonishingly rapid growth in the demand for winter residence, offering a paradise for capitalist speculators. New villas and lodging houses were put up by jobbing builders at breakneck speed. Acquisitive urban landlords snapped up the opportunities for rental income. Almost overnight the town became a kind of 'El Dorado', with rocketing land values and property rents. By the last decade of the century, though, Ventnor had succeeded in turning itself into a stable and prosperous local municipality, well-provided for with public facilities, including a fine array of shops and a medley of charitable enterprises. Once railway communication was established and after the arrival of holidays with pay, the town began to become very popular with summer visitors, following the standard tradition of the English seaside. By and large, this is the town that, in physical terms, early twenty-first century visitors see today. The following pages tease out what made Ventnor so attractive to the Victorians and how relative physical isolation has acted to preserve much of its nineteenth-century ambience. Above all, its distinctive winter climate is once more being appreciated, beginning with the rise of Ventnor's now famous Botanic Gardens, developed from 1972 in the former grounds of the Royal National Hospital, but, much more recently, with the town's growing renaissance as an all-year holiday destination.

Michael Freeman,
Spring Hill, Ventnor,

A view of the town in 2008, taken from aboard a boat in Ventnor Bay

Ventnor, Isle of Wight

The English Mediterranean

'Ventnor hangs upon the side of a steep hill, and here and there it clings and scrambles, is propped up and terraced, like one of the bright-faced little towns that look down upon the Mediterranean' (Henry James)

Panoramas from the sea

Ventnor is a town that defies comparison with most other seaside resorts in Britain, let alone those on the Isle of Wight. Its form is most apparent when viewed from out at sea. In days gone by, you could do this from the end of Ventnor's magnificent iron pier, or from one of the many pleasure steamers that landed visitors to the town. Now it has to be from the deck of one of the power boats that carry visitors across the bay and along the coast towards St.Catherine's Lighthouse. The town is remarkable for the way its buildings are stretched across the steep hillside in ascending ranks of terraces, extending upwards to nearly 400 feet. One hundred years ago, there were many more buildings than there are visible today, and the effect was even more striking. Some structures have been lost to ground movement, for here we are in a major landslip zone. A surprising number were lost to enemy bombing in World War II, while others have been swept away by developers' bulldozers. But what still cannot fail to add to the remarkable vista is the range of downs and cliffs that buttress Ventnor to the north. Rising to nearly 800 feet, they are almost mountainous in elevation, and occasionally mist-capped just like real mountains. The effect is to turn the town into a giant amphitheatre, opening out southward to sun and sea. The sea becomes the stage-set and the rising terraces the seating galleries. It is this very unusual topographical site that in large part explains Ventnor and the Undercliff's distinctive winter climate, one in which all manner of plants can be in bloom in the depths of winter and tiny lizards can be seen basking on south facing walls or rocks on a sunny December day.

Another view of the town, but this time taken from the pier, the date the mid-1890s when many more buildings crowded the ascending terraces

It was above all the Victorians who made Ventnor and they who defined its character in terms of the resorts or watering places with which they thought it most compared. For many it was unambiguously Mediterranean, with its sunlit villas and gardens clambering one upon the other up the steep hill slopes. Nineteenth-century visitors who had vacationed on Italy's Amalfi coast likened it to Positano, a dramatic cliffside resort on the Italian Riviera south of Naples. Other visitors found that Ventnor reminded them of the Swiss resort of Interlaken: the pure air and the startling quality of light made for a life outdoors, a life of walking and excursioning. However, another place with which Ventnor was often compared was the island of Madeira. And the central clue to this particular comparison was the limited diurnal variation in temperature that islands so often demonstrate. Madeira was naturally warmer, relatively speaking, but Ventnor shared with it the ameliorating effects of being surrounded by sea. One enterprising guide- book went so far as to remark that the town had no need to stake claim to being the king or queen of English watering places; it was enough to say it was 'The English Madeira'.

Architects played to these various comparisons in the designs that they chose for Ventnor's remarkable building boom in the middle decades of the nineteenth century. Italianate villas vied with Swiss-style chalets to ornament the successive ledges that provided sites for new residences. Some contemporary commentators claimed that Ventnor displayed examples of almost every known order and style of architecture, with Strawberry Hill Gothic at one extreme and Carpenter's Palazzo at another. The effect, it was often suggested, was motley and ill-favoured. However, Ventnor's Victorian builders were really doing nothing more than what was commonplace across the land. The decades from the 1840s saw a startling variety of architectural experimentation, aided by the much wider availability of building materials like bricks and iron, following the spread of railways.

Examples of such eclecticism can still be seen, despite all the losses to ground movement, wartime bombing and the developer's bulldozer. On the Esplanade, the newly-restored *Villa Amanti* offers perhaps the best surviving example of Italianate work, complete with curved stone internal staircase. Built around 1851, it was once named *Villa Beneditti*, according to early Ventnor guides, and then contained apartments for rent. A little further east, by the Cascade, is *St. Augustine Villa* (1843), Swiss-Italianate in style, set on a rock ledge just above the Esplanade, and arguably one of Ventnor's first and most defining landmarks. At the top of the hillside, the eagle eye may be able to pick out *Ravenscourt* (originally named *Grove Mount*), identified by its crenellated parapet wall. Here, in a commanding site overlooking the bay, is a remarkable Italianate belvedere tower villa, built in local stone about 1840-50, even if the crenellated parapet was a much later addition. A little lower down to the east, on Mitchell Avenue, the eye may also pick out the narrow bellcot tower of the old pumping station. Built in 1883, unambiguously rustic in form, it could be a refugee from a valley in Switzerland.

St. Augustine Villa in about 1890, directly overlooking Ventnor's Royal Victoria Pier

A walk up some of Ventnor's steep zig-zag roads reveals more examples of the indulgence of Ventnor's nineteenth-century architects. At the junction of Grove Road and Spring Hill stands the former *Crab and Lobster Hotel (*later renamed the *King Charles Hotel*), built 1877-8 in grand Italianate style. On St. Boniface Road, Italianate forms re-appear in a number of the pairs of tall villas that flank part of its north side, sometimes interspersed with gothic. Of course, there were some builders and developers who favoured English architectural styles and thus Ventnor inevitably has good surviving examples of the Regency. Higher up Grove Road, for example, one can obtain a sense of what Ventnor was like in its very early days, for here is a series of elegant detached stone villas, mostly 1830-1840, built in a style that might have graced a Bath or a Buxton. The density of building is low and the architectural detailing fine, right down to the filigree ironwork of the verandahs. This was the ambience that early commentators hoped would prevail across the entire town. Unfortunately, Victorian speculators soon ran riot and building plots shrank as land values went skyward.

English Regency on Ventnor's terraces: Yarborough Villa, Grove Road

English Regency is nevertheless apparent in the style chosen for a number of Ventnor's earliest hotels. Today, one of the most striking survivals, viewed from the Esplanade or from the Bay, is the *Wellington*. Half-way along the south side of Belgrave Road, it can be easily identified by the elegant tent-roofed verandahs and cast-iron balustrading of its tall, cream-stuccoed, seaward elevations.

The Wellington Hotel from the Esplanade

Of Ventnor's lost buildings, the most startling has to be the villa built in the style of a gothic folly at the junction of Belgrave and Esplanade Road. It was sheer gothic theatre, a vertical extravaganza on what was already a vertiginous site. Walking the pavement today, one can still pick out remnants of its decorative renderings in the surviving low stone walls.

William Gray's watercolour (1869) of Belgrave Road, gothic villa in centre

The building was erected around 1858 and seems to have ranged over at least three floors. The entire structure was little more than one-room deep and tapered into Esplanade Road. William Gray's painting is dated 1869. It affords quite an accurate architectural rendition, but the vertical positioning is exaggerated, as the rather faded stereoscope photograph below reveals.

Gothic villa, photographed around 1860

The most deeply regretted among Ventnor's lost buildings, though, has to be *Steephill Castle*, the romantic castellated mansion erected by John Hambrough,1833-35. Located on an elevated rock terrace roughly a mile west from the town centre, it enjoyed excellent views across the Channel from many of its principal rooms and from its extensive grounds. When viewed from out at sea, it had the appearance of one of those castles found in fairy tale or fable, a piece of romantic theatre that presented an almost ever-changing image according to the point of the compass from which it was viewed.

Steephill Castle, from a mid-nineteenth century steel engraving

Inside, the castle was renowned for its magnificent oak fittings and for its elaborate wood carvings, although when workmen began demolishing the structure in 1963, they were astonished to find that much of the ornamental woodwork was plaster and much of the oak was actually deal. In its hey-day, it was much frequented by royalty, including Queen Victoria and Prince Albert, the Prince and Princess of Wales, and the Empress of Austria who lived in it during 1874-5. In 1930, the castle was acquired by the Friendship Holidays Association, and, during World War II, served as a local school. By the late 1950s, though, the structure had become unused and dereliction threatened. The list of its practical uses had been exhausted and an order for demolition was obtained. Had it been 30 or 40 years later, the castle would very probably have survived, a vital piece of the Island's heritage and a magnet for tourists.

Approaching the town

Another feature of Ventnor that marks it out from so many other resorts is centred on the routes by which visitors approach it. All offer scenic spectaculars. Today the principal approaches are by road, but one hundred years ago the town boasted two railway connections that also gave visitors a startling introduction to the town's unique topographical site.

Approaching Ventnor from the west, the road today cuts through a long stretch of Undercliff, a luxuriant undergrowth of shrubs and trees, spread over a ground that appears to have been tossed about in almost every direction. The road, too, winds almost uncontrollably as it avoids tumbled masses of rock or sudden declivities, many overshadowed by luxuriant growths of ivy and myrtle. Old man's beard and bindweed seem to be everywhere. Among the glades, wild flowers can be seen in profusion, while in the distance one catches glimpses of the open sea, a blue and silver mirage some 150 to 200 feet below.

*The road through the Undercliff circa 1900; the view
today is surprisingly unaltered*

By the time you reach St.Lawrence, there are signs that this almost tropical wilderness has been tamed. First, picturesque villas, some with viewing towers, peep out from among the tall trees, approached by shaded and damp driveways. Then there is the Botanic Garden on its elongated site just inland from the cliffs. On the road's north side, posh bungalows nestle in extensive gardens, their perimeters lined with all manner of palm trees and other exotic flora. Finally, one reaches the manicured lawns and clipped hedges of Ventnor Park, Victorian to its roots and flanked on the opposite side of the road by a magnificent range of nineteenth-century stone villas, many with their own luxuriant plantings.

Approaching Ventnor from the east, the spectacle could hardly be more different. From Shanklin Old Village, it is an almost continuous ascent as the road climbs around Shanklin Down. The route has an almost alpine character as it tries to trace successive contour lines in a series of horseshoe bends and curves. At almost every turn, the sea is visible to the east and, in places, a magnificent vista opens out northeastward across the whole of Sandown Bay towards the high chalk cliffs at Culver. Rounding the final rising bend near the Luccombe landslip, one's attention is immediately arrested by the sight of the English Channel, extending uninterrupted to the western horizon.

The view of Ventnor from Leeson Road, the spire of Holy Trinity Church right of centre

By now, the road hugs a narrow rock terrace, gently descending to afford a rolling vista of the sea far below. Down Leeson Hill, with its overarching canopy of evergreen oak woods, is one of Ventnor's most notorious hairpin bends (even after substantial road-widening). From here the road drifts downward more gently to become Ventnor High Street and, following the one-way system, takes you along Albert Street to Pier Street and the seaside. But even here, there is still one last scenic drama. With the Winter Gardens building to the left, the road makes a steep descent in two tight hairpins past a series of waterfalls known locally as the Cascade to reach the short Esplanade that was created in 1848 in Ventnor Cove.

A third major route into Ventnor is the one that comes from inland, from Wroxall. It reaches the town through a narrow declivity some 400 feet high up on the down. The undulant overspill settlement of Upper Ventnor suddenly gives way to the much more precipitous cliff settlement of Ventnor proper. Along the aptly named Ocean View Road, the town's buildings cling perilously in descending tiers towards the shore. Past the site of the former main railway station, the road becomes Mitchell Avenue and descends past *Hillside Hotel*, one of Ventnor's earliest, to Spring Hill and the High Street.

A final route to the town was laid out in 1890 with the completion of the new Whitwell road (very recently upgraded). It approaches Ventnor from the west along the inland clifftop, reaching the town proper half-way up Gills Cliff Road. The route is remarkable for the fine semi-continuous view of the sea that it affords on clear days, as well as the panorama of the Undercliff below.

It almost goes without saying that these various road approaches to the town are relatively modern. Visitors in the mid-nineteenth century faced negotiating different and more tortuous routeways, not helped by their reliance on the horse and carriage which always made gradients problematic. Often journeys involved using the traditional 'shutes' that litter many upland parts of the Island. Literally meaning steep hills, they relied for the most part on routes that were gifts of nature as distinct from the more artificial roadways that later engineers carved from cliffsides. Coming to Ventnor from the east, for instance, there was no Leeson Road, merely the steep and narrow White Shute (Bonchurch Shute) that brought you to Ventnor by way of Bonchurch village and its picturesque pond. From the north, from inland locations, there was no Ocean View Road, but, instead, what is now called Old Shute, a more direct but much more precipitous descent to the rock terrace below. From the west, there was merely a narrow trackway leading from Niton, and then a steep shute down from Whitwell and High Hat into St. Lawrence.

Before new roads were made, you could evade these difficulties by entering Ventnor by train. The first line reached the town from Shanklin and Wroxall in 1866, the second from Merstone and Godshill in 1900. The first and principal route burrowed three-quarters of a mile through St. Boniface Down to emerge in a stone quarry, 284 feet above sea-level. Henry de Vere Stacpoole, the novelist and inhabitant of Bonchurch, memorably described how you got on a train at Ryde Pier at sea level and, half an hour later, got out at Ventnor at sky-level, or, at least, half-way up to the clouds. Outside the station, your eye then alighted upon a little town that appeared, in Stacpoole's words, to be trying to leave for Italy, its buildings arranged in steep terraces facing onto a clear blue sea.

Ventnor's main railway station around the turn of the last century,
with elegantly dressed ladies walking along the platform to the exit

The later railway into Ventnor entered from the west, with its terminus behind Steephill Castle, just above Ventnor Park. Like its competitor, this line also burrowed through the downs, but High Hat tunnel was much the shorter and there then followed an extended run eastward at the base of the cliff-face with panoramic views of the Undercliff and the English Channel beyond. When John Betjeman travelled on the line in the days when it was part of the Southern Railway, he was mesmerized by the sight that sprang upon the passenger as the little train emerged from the tunnel in the cliff face above St. Lawrence. The meadows and streams of inland Wight suddenly gave way to something much more exotic. The Undercliff vegetation appeared to have elements of the Amazon jungle about it. Betjeman could not understand why the railway managers did not put observation cars on the branch. Certainly engine drivers appreciated the wonderful vista that greeted unsuspecting passengers as trains emerged from the tunnel face, for they often stopped the locomotive for a few minutes to allow the scene to be absorbed. Sadly, these two approaches to Ventnor are no more. The Ventnor West line was closed as early as 1952 and the main branch in 1966, much to the dismay of the town's commercial interests. However, Ventnor Heritage Museum has working models of both lines and one can walk part of the abandoned course of the Ventnor West branch where it runs at the base of the cliff beneath the Whitwell Road. The buildings of Ventnor West station also survive as private housing in Castle Close and the entrance to High Hat tunnel can be glimpsed from the start of St. Rhadagund's footpath.

Ventnor West station not long before closure

Ventnor as 'El Dorado'

Like many Victorian towns, Ventnor was an 'upstart' creation, for as early guide-books often remarked, the town had no history. It grew on the back of capitalist speculation and on credit. Before 1830, it consisted of nothing more than a few low thatched fishermen's huts, situated on the shore of Ventnor Cove. Their inhabitants gained a living from catching crab and lobster and selling them on to mainland markets. Nearby, a cascade or waterfall tumbled down from a rocky promontory on which a small corn mill stood. A little further up the hillside, at the bottom of what is now Spring Hill, was an ancient, low-timbered, wayside inn, appropriately named the *Crab and Lobster*. But, save for another accommodation inn at the base of the down, the Manor House belonging to Ventnor Farm, and a few more scattered dwellings, Ventnor was otherwise an untamed yet picturesque wilderness, isolated from much of the rest of the Island and difficult of access in almost every direction. It was more often observed and perhaps more often reached from the sea. The town's runaway expansion followed in the wake of the sale in 1828 of the estate that comprised the land upon which Ventnor was eventually built. But the prime catalyst was the publication in 1830 of the second edition of Sir James Clark's treatise on the influence of climate in the prevention and cure of chronic disease. Clark was later a physician to Queen Victoria and his book incorporated a comparative eulogy on the relative merits for invalids of the various watering places of the south of England. Clark was astonished that the unique advantages of Ventnor, in point of shelter and position, had been for so long overlooked. The area of the Undercliff was especially well protected from winter cold. In effect, Clark offered a blueprint for a winter health resort that had the capacity to exceed all

The Undercliff today, viewed from above St. Lawrence, with Ventnor just visible in the left middle distance

Almost overnight, Ventnor became a magnet for speculators, riding high on Clark's effusive endorsement of the salubrity of the winter air. According to a local diarist, Mark Norman, the nascent town became spoken of far and wide as another 'El Dorado'. All sorts of conditions of men rushed to the site in seek of fortune. Among them were builders without capital or credit or character, speculators who never raised a profit, and all manner of other adventurers. Flashy firms, so Mark Norman recorded, would come down from London in a blaze of publicity, walk through the quagmires of mud in their sheepskin gaiters and with their measuring rods, only later to collapse into bankruptcy, leaving local tradesmen and lodgings owners with a host of unpaid bills. The place was rapidly infested with jerry builders who ran up houses of inferior order, mortgaged them, then failed to keep up their payments, whereupon the houses fell into the hands of lawyers. There was a singular absence of ready money. All that was in circulation were scores of promissory notes. Norman recorded how it was a standing joke in the town in the later 1830s that there was only one five pound note in circulation. Even so, land prices and ground rents rocketed. Plots that sold in 1830 for £100 an acre were fetching four times the figure within little more than a decade. In the choicest spots, prices rose to as much as £1000. The quip was that Ventnor was becoming as expensive a place to live as Mayfair. As building work progressed, the neighbourhood became honeycombed with quarries, carved out of the local greensand. Roads, hitherto never more than tracks, were quickly cut up into deep gullies from the continual passage of builders' carts. In wet weather, they turned into swamps. The route that was later to become High Street vanished into ploughed fields near the site of the present Ventnor Brewery. So much building work was in progress that there was a dearth of foliage or greenery, creating a scene that was a far cry from the salubrious winter resort that Sir James Clark had envisaged.

The capitalists who flocked to Ventnor to run up a quick profit were fundamentally interested in building lodging houses and villas that would prove attractive for invalids seeking the curative powers of Ventnor's genial climate in coping with pulmonary disease. As one later town guide remarked, Sir James Clark's eulogy had set the whole world of invalids in motion: they began descending upon the makeshift settlement in droves. Yet there was a chronic shortage of accommodation for visitors and it was this that offered a speculator's paradise. In September 1844, an advertisement in *The Times* gave details of eligible villa residences in the course of completion near the entrance to the town. Boarding house proprietors up and down the land were encouraged to consider having 'branch establishments' in Ventnor as an up and coming watering place. The gothic style villas were positioned along St. Boniface Road, south-facing and with a commanding view of the sea. All were plainly built as a speculation. A few years before, in 1841, *The Times* had given notice of a bankruptcy sale for Grove House and Lodge just west of St. Catherine's Church. This was another newly-built gothic-style villa, located in one of Ventnor's prime sites. But what made this newspaper entry the more interesting was the assertion that the air in Ventnor assimilated to the mild climate of the island of Madeira. And this was the perception that, repeatedly, over the course of the nineteenth century, drew speculative investors, acquisitive landlords, invalids and ordinary visitors alike to flock to the town. Even the local parsonage, built on the site of the modern Winter Gardens, was rented out for visitors, for in October 1862, *The Times* carried an advertisement describing its ample accommodation, with an excellent paid cook, available for £130 in the six winter months or £210 for the entire year.

Regardless of the loss of many Victorian buildings, few of those walking the streets of Ventnor today can fail to register the force of its past history as a resort for invalids, in winter especially. Several decades before holidays with pay and before the railways brought hordes of ordinary people in summer to experience the English seaside, Ventnor already had its tiers and ranks of boarding houses. Extending over three or four floors, they were rented out both as sets of rooms and as entire houses, in the latter case accommodating not just the family but its servants as well. Surviving bill-heads emphasize the distinctions between winter and summer visitors. The latter were charged for the familiar 'board residence', typically staying on a week by week basis. Winter visitors, by contrast, had private sitting rooms to go with their bedrooms, indicative of very much longer stays.

The special feature of the array of Ventnor's boarding establishments was that they catered for the full variety of the resort's ailing and sick visitors. The most delicate patients could reside where the situation was mildest and sunniest, universally recognized as being along Belgrave Road or the terraces immediately below. Patients of a more robust constitution could stay higher up along Grove Road, Spring Hill or along St. Boniface Terrace. Here the air was more bracing and there were ample opportunities for walking the downs. Local physicians soon developed an expert knowledge of the relative merits of different sites for patients in different stages of pulmonary disease. Often they encouraged patients to move their lodgings as the severity of their medical conditions advanced. Invariably this meant moving down towards the bay with its warmer and more sheltered conditions. In 1849, the local physican, Dr. George Martin, summarized many of the locality's merits as a place of winter resort in a widely-read book on the Undercliff of the Island. He described the 'invalid' months as extending from the beginning of October to the end of June or July.

An early view of the eastern end of the Esplanade. The tower of St. Augustine Villa is visible behind the hotel, while to the right, perched on the cliff, is the former Vicarage, now the Winter Gardens.

With its many invalids, not to mention other well-off visitors, Ventnor quickly developed an extensive livery service, with various establishments supplying horses, vehicles, coachmen and grooms on a hire basis. Among them, Jackmans seems to have been able to procure any type of vehicle on demand and could always find additional horses when needed. There were also pony carts for hire in the town, used especially for getting between the Esplanade and the High Street.

High Street, Ventnor.

The top end of High Street circa 1900, the former spire of St. Catherine's Church in the middle distance (it had to be dismantled as unsafe in 1921). Today, the view is even more changed. The buildings to the immediate left have disappeared, the buildings to the immediate right remain but have ceased to be shops, while the road has been widened to form a short dual carriageway.

The town's early history as a winter resort remains very apparent today in terms of the long sequence of shops that line its central thoroughfares, some now empty or given over to charitable uses. In fact, the full range of establishments was greater in the nineteenth century than one sees today, for shops lined the bottom of Spring Hill and the north side of the High Street at the point where the main shoppers' car park is currently found. Some of these premises were lost to bombing in the 1939-45 war; others have gone in redevelopment. In late Victorian times, Ventnor was reckoned to have the best shopping of any of the Island's towns. By 1891, one town guide even remarked that its shops were as 'numerous and of a class which one would look for in a leading provincial town'. At one stage, there were no less than four chemists, as clear an illustration of the town's invalid clientèle as one might expect to find. There were also purveyors of all kinds of mineral waters, some utilizing local spring sources.

One of the town's earliest chemist shops, providing 'accurate dispensing' and 'invalids' requisites'. The shop eventually became the chemist Boots.

Alongside boarding houses and shops, Ventnor soon acquired a series of hotels, used by wealthier visitors. Some grew from the earliest Ventnor villas, especially the ones positioned in the choicest spots above the bay. Prize among them was the *Marine Hotel* on Belgrave Road, built in 1839, with unrivalled views out over the bay and an easy walk to the High Street. Among its guests were English and foreign royalty and in 1886 it became the *Royal Marine Hotel.* There were wealthy visitors, including many from continental Europe, who stayed in the hotel year after year, such was the quality of its accommodation and service. By 1900 it offered to visitors the facility of electric light, a lift, telephone and central heating. It maintained kitchen gardens in what is now The Grove car park. Further west on the same road, though set back from the cliff, was the almost equally grand *Royal Hotel*, opened in 1832. This establishment survives today in much extended form, whereas the *Royal Marine* was closed in 1937 and the building subsequently lost to bombing in the 1939-45 war. Away from the seafront terraces, at the bottom of Spring Hill, the *Crab and Lobster Hotel* boasted in 1905 that it had electric light throughout, heated corridors, a hotel omnibus that met all arriving trains and that French was spoken in the establishment. The popularity of Ventnor among well-off visitors from continental Europe was underlined by the Ventnor guides that incorporated sections translated into both French and German.

The Royal Marine Hotel on Belgrave Road, circa 1910

The chaos of Ventnor's earliest development did not prevent the erection of a number of public buildings. John Hambrough, builder of nearby Steephill Castle, endowed St. Catherine's Church, a parsonage and schools, the church consecrated in 1837. The church remains a prominent landmark today, significantly extended from its original design, but without its steeple. The parsonage stood on the cliff east of the Cascade, a commodious structure in stone and slate which eventually became much admired for its beautiful garden full of tamarisk trees. Later, in 1844, leading townsmen secured an Act of Parliament for town improvements. The Esplanade was constructed across the cove in 1848, a new high road built east out of the town high above Bonchurch village, several of the old shutes lowered, and the perilous trackway up from behind the *Royal Hotel* to what is now Ocean View Road was re-made to form the present Zig Zag Road. Even so, there were still commentators writing in the early twentieth century who wondered how a town could ever have been built on so precipitous a site. By then there were yet more zig-zag roads, as well as many sets of steps, to the extent that, in one writer's view, steps and zig-zags became to Ventnor what canals were to Venice. Some of the gradients are as steep as one in four, a feature that the hordes of ordinary summer holidaymakers soon cursed as they trudged with their suitcases up Grove Road to reach the main railway station to return home on Saturdays. It was no wonder that there were various projects floated for a funicular railway connecting the main station with the beach far below.

The sunniest of spots

Ventnor regularly features as one of the sunniest resorts in Britain, and conspicuously so in the winter months. In some years it has stood at the head of the list of sunshine records. However, this has rarely meant that Ventnor suffers from excessive summer heat. In the first instance, the summer sun rises and sets behind downs, so that the resort gets some two hours less sunshine each day than similar south-facing coastal towns. Secondly, the proximity of the sea and the island situation ensure that summer heat waves are nearly always moderated by onshore breezes. It is this same proximity that ensures that excessive cold is also moderated, for sea surface temperatures around Britain show only limited variation with the seasons. The result is that Ventnor enjoys a remarkably limited diurnal temperature range. In 1901, for example it was 10.38F; in 2008, it was 9.75F. Rainfall affords another meteorological aspect in which Ventnor ranks favourably. The annual average is quite low for England, at around 28 inches. But equally important is the fact that there is a tendency for that rain to fall more often during the night than during the day, so that there is a perception that the resort is drier still. However, the key to understanding Ventnor's nineteenth-century growth and prosperity is to be found in its distinctive *winter* climate. And this, of course, was the feature that most exercised Sir James Clark in terms of its potential benefit for invalids. In England, the low angle of the sun in the winter means that little heat is generated by its rays. In Ventnor, however, the Undercliff's unique topography, comprising a series of south-facing, seaward-slanting terraces and a cliff face immediately behind, results in the sun's rays falling more directly on the land surface and the intercepted heat becoming trapped. As Dr. John Whitehead, a local meteorological observer remarked in 1881, this gave rise to a mean daily temperature range in winter (based on 40 years of continuous recording) of just 7.1 degrees Fahrenheit. This was five or six degrees less than inland sites on the mainland. Today much the same figures apply. On sunny days, modern visitors will not fail to notice how sheltered spots along the beach or on the terraces above quickly develop a quite unseasonal warmth. In the nineteenth century, this was where the serried ranks of verandahs that graced so many of Ventnor's buildings really came into their own. Whilst they plainly offered shelter from the sun's heat in summer, they helped in winter to add to the heat trap that the Undercliff already provided. So on sunny January days, French doors would be opened and visitors offered a taste of the Mediterranean. It was no vain boast in the nineteenth century that Ventnor had a mean January air temperature that was higher than that of parts of Italy and Greece.

The evidence that most often confirmed to nineteenth-century visitors that Ventnor had a unique *winter* climate lay in the astonishing variety of plants that could be observed in flower even in the coldest of weeks. This feature remains equally true today, as a wander through Ventnor's now famous Botanic Gardens will reveal. Fuschias and geraniums often bloom throughout the season, some growing almost into trees. In some years, the hawthorn flowers at Christmas, as do many spring bulbs. When Ventnor was at its most fashionable as a winter resort, residents and visitors would write to the editor of *The Times* and describe the range of plants in flower on their garden terraces. One described the Christmas weather in 1880 when there were four different kinds of roses in bloom, along with veronicas of every shade, double stocks, French marguerites, cyclamen, scarlet geranium, together with primroses and violets in profusion. Visitors to Ventnor's Botanic Gardens are often astounded at the way, in some years, shrubs and perennials can still be in full flower in a December or a January. Nor is it at all unusual to find plants like red-hot pokers in almost continuous bloom in sheltered corners on the terraces above Ventnor Bay or in the Cascade garden. But it is not just the extension of the flowering season that is the clue to Ventnor's unusual climate. What is also central is the range of 'exotics' that seem to thrive in the Undercliff. It is not merely the variety of palm trees that impress visitors, but the range of Mediterranean plants, including succulents, that may be seen growing. When he first visited Ventnor in the later 1940s, John Betjeman was so enthralled by the areas of garden full of exotics that he almost expected to see a bird of paradise flitting from bloom to bloom. The famous Bonchurch novelist, Henry de Vere Stacpoole, came to much the same observation. In the Botanic Gardens, there are areas dedicated to plants from warmer climes, the South African and Mediterranean terraces forming perhaps the most remarkable of them. When the garden formed part of the grounds of the Royal National Hospital, it is easy to understand how patients were able to describe sunny days in February as just like summer. Even when the predominant air stream was a cold one, a few hours of sunshine could raise temperatures to quite unseasonal levels. The same remains true, of course, today.

Ventnor viewed from near Flowers Brook - a Raphael Tuck postcard image from a watercolour by H.E. Wimbush, circa 1900

The sea, the sea

Ventnor's earliest inhabitants, as we have remarked, gained their livelihood from fishing, especially for crab and lobster. But with the rise of the town as a winter health resort and, in later decades, as a mass summer holiday destination, the sea at Ventnor took on a very different significance. Visitors were to be seen spending many hours lying or sitting on the beach on bright days. The more able-bodied spent their time searching for the famous 'Ventnor diamonds', tiny pieces of transparent quartz that glittered in the sun. Others searched the surrounding rocks for geological specimens which they could take to a shop in the High Street for further identification. On the Esplanade itself, there were premises offering hot and cold sea-water baths. Meanwhile the growing contemporary craze for sea-bathing soon saw the line above high-water mark crowded with commodious bathing-machines, carefully separated for male and female use. However, most guide-books were quick to remark on the steeply-shelving nature of the beach and the strength of the backwash, both of which could catch the inexperienced bather unawares. Longshoremen's boats offered visitors trips around the bay and there were also rowing and sailing boats to be hired, although it was essential to watch out for sunken rocks and rip currents. Today, in 2009, visitors can observe these last features first-hand. At low states of the tide, a long reef can be seen exposed some 50 metres from the high water mark, while towards high water a strong swell can sometimes develop that makes bathing hazardous, even when wind conditions do not appear especially strong .

No part of this coast offers any natural harbour and it is no surprise to find that, as the town grew, there were ideas of constructing one: not just for bringing in goods like coal and timber, but to provide a landing place for the many pleasure steamers that increasingly plied this portion of the south coast in the summer season. Although an early unsuccessful attempt to make a landing place was tried in the 1840s, the first major project involved the construction of two breakwaters, the western one extending south and east to a length of 600 feet, the eastern one extending in a south-westerly direction for 300 feet. Together they were to form a refuge harbour, with an entrance some 180 feet wide. Work commenced in 1863 and within a short time the western breakwater was of a sufficient length to allow its use as a steamer pier at high water. However, one steamer, the *Chancellor*, made the mistake of berthing on a falling tide and its hull was punctured, rendering the vessel immoveable. Then, in a subsequent storm, the vessel's moorings broke and she was thrown broadside on to the beach to become a total wreck. It was to prove an unhappy omen. Construction of the western breakwater was resumed, nevertheless, and by the summer of 1864 a regular steamer service was established to and from Littlehampton for trains to London. Pleasure steamers from Portsmouth and Southampton also began making calls. That autumn, however, parts of the eastern breakwater then under construction were destroyed in a series of fierce storms and some damage was also sustained to the western arm. Further storm damage occurred in 1865 and by autumn of the following year, large portions of the project were in ruins. The central problem had been the method of construction: timber piles in two parallel lines, infilled with stone, rock and soil. In storm conditions, the sea readily scoured out the infill, leaving only a timber skeleton. By early 1867, the only option left was for the harbour remains to be sold and dismantled.

Ventnor's short-lived refuge harbour

In 1866, the railway had reached Ventnor, affording the town a much easier means of supplying heavy, bulky commodities like coal, iron and timber, so the merits of a harbour became less pressing. Instead, a number of townsmen began plans for an iron pier, following the pattern of many seaside towns of the day. Construction commenced in 1871 and by August 1872 it extended to 200 feet, sufficient to prompt the promoters to arrange a public opening. By September the following year, the pier had grown to 478 feet and all that remained to be completed was the pierhead and the landing stage. However, the pier company's supply of capital had by now been exhausted and it proved difficult to raise new funds. Not until the late summer of 1881 was a landing stage completed, a full ten years on from the start of the project. Unfortunately for the pier's promoters, though, their creation had a very short life. A fierce November storm that year wrecked the new landing stage and took away part of the pier neck. Then, in the autumn of 1882, the pier sustained yet further storm damage. There was no alternative except to begin again. The task was taken on by the Local Board which obtained a new Act and work eventually commenced in 1885. Winter storms again hampered progress, but the pier was finally opened for steamer traffic by the summer of 1887. In the first full excursion season, 1888, some 10,000 passengers disembarked, providing Ventnor with much new business. Large saloon steamers soon plied daily in summer to and from Bournemouth, Southsea, Shanklin and Sandown. The pier, when completed had a bandstand at its head, but in 1903 this was removed to Ventnor Park and replaced in 1907 by a pavilion suitable for concerts and other sorts of performances. A new bandstand was later added to the pavilion's front, facing the Esplanade. In the years before the Great War, military bands played here on most evenings.

A view of the pier taken in the 1920s

An 1892 guide-book to the island was unambiguous about the attractiveness of Ventnor's new 600 feet seaside addition. Named the *Royal Victoria Pier*, it was described as a 'light, graceful, almost airy structure', with ornamental screens of glass and timber along its length, providing shelter from strong winds and from glaring sun. From the pierhead, one now obtained a glorious panorama of Ventnor's unique topographic position, the green bulk of St. Boniface Down towering over the extensive terraces of buildings below.

Today, as visitors will quickly register, there is no pier to be seen. The structure had been extensively renewed following the 1939-45 war, after a survey revealed it to be unsafe. The government footed much of the cost, since part of the neck of the pier had been removed as a defence measure early on in the war. The new structure was 683 feet long and had a reinforced concrete pierhead that incorporated an entertainment complex and sun deck. When opened in 1955, it became the most modern pier in Britain. In its concert hall, visitors could listen daily to Bill Donachie at the pier's mighty Hammond Organ. They could dance and sing every afternoon and evening. There was a licensed bar and refreshment facilities. Unhappily, winter storms over subsequent decades, a disastrous fire in 1985, along with more general corrosion, steadily affected the structure's integrity. The landing stages had been found to be in a poor state as early as the late 1960s and, faced with a decline in numbers of visiting pleasure steamers, it was decided not to renew them as they decayed. The pier itself was repaired from time to time, but as with so many others like it, the costs of maintenance seemed to escalate uncontrollably. Various ideas were put forward for its replacement. One envisaged a jettied breakwater, while another involved the construction of a kind of mini-pier. However, the former was abandoned over issues of coastal engineering and the latter foundered through lack of funds. Finally, in the 1990s, the pier ended up in the hands of the demolition contractor and now hardly any trace of it survives. However, with the help of European funding, Ventnor subsequently acquired a small harbour, *Ventnor Haven*, opened in 2003. In broad shape though not in scale, it is reminiscent of the abortive harbour scheme of the 1860s, but its breakwaters are this time constructed of rock, not of timber. However, the harbour is tidal and requires repeated scouring of sand and seaweed to maintain it. Moreover, it is suitable for use only by very small vessels and can be approached in a strong south-easterly only at some risk.

Ventnor Haven, completed in 2003

Municipal prosperity

By the final decades of the nineteenth century and up until the outbreak of World War I, Ventnor displayed all the signs of a vigorous and prosperous town, powerfully conscious of its identity. Not only did it have a still expanding range of shops, but it also boasted many of the other facilities that became such important hallmarks of Victorian life. The town had several newspapers, among them the *Isle of Wight Mercury*, founded in 1855[1]. A Literary and Scientific Institute had been established in the High Street, in which were found a free library, reading room and lecture hall. In the autumn and spring of each year, Oxford University Extension lectures were held there. In parallel, there was Knight's Circulating Library, Book Saloon and Pianoforte and Music warehouse at 147-9 High Street. By 1908 it had almost 12,000 books that could be borrowed for a small fee. In Albert Street, there was erected a capacious assembly room (originally called the Undercliff Assembly Rooms and renamed the Town Hall in 1900) set behind a grand classically-inspired portico. All manner of concerts, shows, bazaars and exhibitions were staged there. On the Esplanade, there was the Ventnor Pavilion, erected 1896, where during both winter and summer all kinds of entertainments were laid on, including the town's first moving picture show around 1912. The Pavilion was built in oriental style, with an octagonal central viewing lantern, surmounted by a fine cupola. It had seating for at least 500 people. Just west of the main town, a large public garden and recreation ground was maintained, becoming known as Ventnor Park. At first it was merely leased from the Hambrough estate, but the Council was able to buy it outright, together with a section of the western cliffs, in 1910. In summer, illuminated promenade concerts were eventually staged there. Parts of the town were lighted by gas from as early as 1851 and unlimited water supplies were drawn from various natural springs emanating from the base of the chalk downs. Electricity first came in 1899, although some gas lamps remained in use after World War Two.

Ventnor Park – an inter-war view

Sports and related pastimes had also become well catered for in Ventnor by the close of the Victorian era. There were Undercliff Cricket and Football Clubs, with grounds at Steephill.

---

[1] The paper continued in publication right up to the mid-1980s, having amalgamated with the *Isle of Wight Advertiser* in 1923. The town is now served by the *South Wight Chronicle,* established in 1991.

There was an Undercliff Swimming Club, with a bathing house at Myrtle Bay. The recreation ground at Ventnor Park accommodated tennis courts and a bowling green. Golfers found a 'capital' nine-hole course on Rew Downs, where visitors were welcome. Then there was the annual Regatta and the annual Carnival. The latter was always an extraordinary event, quite out of proportion to the size of the town and acquiring celebrity far beyond the Island.

The townspeople's spiritual needs, as well as those of visitors, were also exceptionally well provided for by the close of the nineteenth century. A second Anglican church, Holy Trinity, to the designs of C.E. Giles, was erected in 1861-2 in Trinity Road. With its thin160-foot spire, it remains a notable landmark, especially when seen from the downs above. Closer to the town centre, in the High Street, there was a large Congregational Church, erected on the site of a smaller chapel in 1854 and enlarged further in 1872. One guide-book described it as a building with considerable architectural pretensions and it could accommodate as many as 650 people. A Catholic Church, St. Wilfrid's, was completed in Trinity Road in 1871. Alongside these principal places of worship, Ventnor also boasted a Wesleyan Chapel, a Baptist Chapel, a Primitive Methodist, a Bible Christian and a meeting house for Plymouth Brethren.

The former Congregational Church on High Street

Charitable organizations and works were also, of course, a key feature of Victorian life and society and Ventnor inhabitants afforded no exception. The Royal National Hospital for

Consumption and Diseases of the Chest, opened in 1869 on the St.Lawrence Road about a mile west of the town, relied heavily on charitable giving for its operation. As the first national institution of its type, it had a very wide range of charitable support, with an office in London and the benefit of royal endorsement. However, it is clear that it also drew much support locally, both from the town's permanent residents and from its long-term winter visitors. A patient at the hospital in early 1877 remarked how townspeople were frequent visitors, helping with entertainments and benefit concerts. Some were of a very fashionable class, if nearly all invalids, although this did not appear to diminish the measure of their enthusiasm. A related charitable body was the Ventnor Relief Fund, founded 1873, which existed to provide financial support to former patients of the Royal National Hospital who wished to remain in Ventnor to continue their recovery.

For some consumptives in advanced states of the disease, Ventnor, sadly, became a place to die and in 1879 a charity was formed to help cater for their plight. St. Catherine's Home for Patients of Advanced Consumption was established at Peake House, Grove Road, as an outcome. It could take 12 in-patients. Extensions were carried out in the 1890s, including a mortuary chapel, and in the early twentieth century the Home acquired several adjacent properties. By then it had also started to admit children, especially those with chest complaints and, in effect, became a boarding school.

St. Catherine's Home in Grove Road

Another convalescent home for consumptives was to be found in Madeira Road towards Bonchurch. It was managed by the Royal Hants County Hospital, but supported mainly by voluntary contributions. The London City Mission also maintained a seaside home on the Newport road in Ventnor, intended for use by its missionaries, recuperating after their arduous exertions, although a small number of consumptive patients was sometimes accommodated.

If one searches for the evidence of Ventnor's municipal life of one hundred years ago, it soon becomes clear there is much that has vanished. The Congregational Church on the High Street was demolished in 1986, even after re-building following extensive bomb damage in World War Two. Part of a transept and various memorial stones are all that remain of this once imposing structure, visible at the rear of the High Street car park. Opposite it, a string of shops and cottages have been swept away, to be replaced by a four and five-storey block of council flats that must stake claim to forming one of modern Ventnor's worst post-war eyesores, a structure entirely out of scale and out of character with everything around it.

The Undercliff Assembly Rooms (later the Town Hall), had to be demolished in the 1990s, by then far too costly to repair following two fires, but its street facade was saved in the re-building. The former Literary and Scientific Institute happily survives today as Ventnor Library. The Royal National Hospital escaped the German bombs, but succumbed instead to the march of science, notably antibiotic medicine. By the early 1960s it had become superfluous and, when searches for alternative uses failed, it fell to the bulldozer in 1969, although some of the hospital chapel's fabulous stained glass was saved and installed in nearby St. Lawrence Church. The hospital's extensive grounds were to acquire new life as a botanic garden. After some forty years of development, it is now internationally known and a jewel among the Island's visitor attractions, ranked alongside Osborne House and Brading Roman Villa. St. Catherine's Home, with its striking chapel tower in French gothic, happily remains an arresting sight as one walks down the steep hill from Mitchell Avenue or upward from Grove Road's junction with Spring Hill. Sadly, though, the building's southern elevation has been ruined by modern extensions. The Home is now a school for children with special needs. On the Esplanade, modern visitors are often amazed to learn that Blake's beach huts are relics of the old bathing machines that once used to be hauled up and down the beach more than a century ago. Ventnor Park remains very much intact, even if some of its sports facilities have gone elsewhere. Finally, perhaps one of the most startling instances of continuity between past and present is represented by the Ventnor Carnival. Started in 1889, it has survived with few interruptions for well over a century and remains a powerful symbol of community identity that continues to give pleasure to generations of adults and children alike.

'While I breathe I hope'[2]

The Royal National Hospital had a working life of nearly a hundred years and no account of Ventnor's history would be complete without some specific reference to its nature and purpose[3]. Today, when visitors drive into the elongate parking area for Ventnor Botanic Garden, they are on the site of the hospital buildings which stretched out in a single long line parallel to the road and the coastal cliff. Standing in the car park, it is no longer immediately

---

[2] A translation from the latin 'Dum spiro spero', the motto found in Block 8 of the hospital
[3] The institution was initially known as the National Cottage Hospital for Consumption.

apparent how close the site is to the sea, for trees and shrubs have grown up on the cliff brow. But one hundred years ago, this part of the Undercliff was much more open and most of the hospital bedrooms had panoramic views across the English Channel.

Consumption, or what later became known as Tuberculosis, was a highly prevalent disease in the nineteenth century. It could also be slow and lingering in form. Roughly a fifth of Victorian adult mortality was normally accounted for by it. For the most part, consumptive patients were excluded from general hospitals. Instead, they were housed in large institutions outside of towns and cities where various efforts were made to 'manage' the disease. It was already the view of a number of distinguished physicians that better results could be obtained by removing patients to locations by the sea and this, as we have seen, was the basis of Ventnor's early runaway growth. The chest hospital at Ventnor was the specific brainchild of Dr. Arthur Hill Hassall (b. 1817) and the broad plan was to make treatment available to a much wider body of the population than just those who had the means to take winter lodgings in the resort, or other resorts like it. However, the hospital was not designed around having large wards for patients. It was established instead on what was called the 'cottage principle' and there was an emphasis on separation. Patients were to be housed in a series of small buildings, each with no more than six patients, each building having its principal rooms facing sun and sea, and surrounded by gardens. The 'cottages' were to have sitting rooms as well as individual sleeping rooms, together with all the other conveniences of an ordinary home. Temperature was regulated by means of special systems of heating and ventilation and all patients had access to covered south-facing verandahs where they were encouraged to sit out on all but the worst of days.

One of the hospital blocks housing women patients

Ultimately, there were 10 such blocks, together with a central service block, including kitchens and large communal dining room, and a separate chapel. The central service block was unusual in having the kitchens at the top of the building, ensuring that all steam and smells were ventilated straight to the outside air. In time, there were 132 beds in total, with separate quarters for men and women. Construction began in 1868 and continued intermittently for much of the succeeding decades, the first patients being admitted in 1869. The architectural style of the buildings was something of a mixture. The Chapel was perpendicular gothic, while the main buildings were largely Tudor but with some gothic motifs, coupled with a French pavilion tower. All the buildings were in the local Ventnor stone and made for an impressive facade when viewed from the roadside to the north.

An aerial view of the Royal National Hospital, showing its sheltered site in the Undercliff, with the sea shore just visible at the base of the cliffs

Patients described the conditions in the hospital in their letters home. Many were overcome by the beauty of the place and by the way they were allowed to do what they liked. The more seriously ill were put on what was called a 'two-hour diet', that is sustinence at two-hour intervals over the course of the day. This included milk and eggs, beef tea, fresh meat, and port wine and biscuits at supper time. You could actually lay in bed and watch the sea, or, if health and weather permitted, be taken out for a drive in an invalid's carriage drawn by a donkey. For the rather less seriously ill, there was a library and a harmonium to play, as well as opportunities for indoor games like bagatelle. One could also go for a walk in the gardens. Thomas Fry was admitted to the hospital early in 1877 aged around 26 and wrote regularly to his parents recording the progress of his treatment. He dined off milk and bacon, stewed steak, roast beef, and rice and marmalade puddings. Even if your appetite was not very good, there always seemed to be something tasty on the table. The servants and nursing staff were kind, the chaplain, when he came round, 'a nice old boy'. Although it was February, there were some days of very fine weather, almost like summer, when they went on outings. Already he felt that his condition was improving. There were six patients in his particular cottage and he described them as the 'jolliest' in the place. He reckoned that he would perish laughing if he did not get fat on the food and fresh air. Thomas was discharged from the hospital later in 1877 and, together with his family, emigrated to Australia in 1881. He survived there until 1915, perhaps testament to the hospital's care in his younger days.

The Royal National Hospital, or RNH as it typically came to be known, provided no cure for tuberculosis prior to the introduction of antibiotics in the 1950s. However, the hospital's surviving annual medical reports reveal something of its efficacy in managing the symptoms of the disease. In 1901, for example, 756 patients were discharged, all of them improved in some degree. Alongside, there had been eight deaths and 99 patients who were either worse or unchanged.

Old Manor House Tea Garden, shortly before the Great War, a visual record of a world that was shortly to disappear for all time

War clouds were already heavy on the horizon for some months before war broke out early in August 1914. The German bands that had frequented Ventnor and other resorts had returned home, as had German waiters. Many of the town's regular foreign visitors, including many Germans of course, had also revised their vacation plans, with the result that beach and Esplanade had already begun to look unseasonal. By the August Bank Holiday, steamer excursions were being curtailed, as were excursion trips arriving by rail. In common with cities and towns up and down the country, Ventnor was soon witness to recruiting drives, typically in the form of open-air public meetings addressed by prominent local men. By 1915, men and horses were everywhere leaving to join regiments. The town's Fire Brigade had seen 18 of its 20 member team go off to fight by February of that year. The town's various women's organizations were soon arranging working parties to supply so-called 'comforts' for the troops overseas. As the fighting across the Channel intensified, so Ventnor (and St. Lawrence) became a receiving centre for the wounded.

The cessation of Ventnor's normal resort trade, both in summer and winter seasons, had dramatic effects upon the town's prosperity. Hotels saw their visitor lists much reduced. Lodging and boarding houses were increasingly empty for long periods. Several well-known shops were forced to close their doors through the collapse of trade. Some towns were able to compensate for such losses by being primary points for the billeting of troops, but Ventnor largely lost out on this facility. By 1916 it was being granted £1500 in relief from the Government War Fund as a direct outcome. Later in 1916, the town at last had some success in being selected to provide housing for soldiers, but for some of the town's businesses it was too little too late. On the Esplanade, one positive change was the turning over of Ventnor Pavilion to the making of aeroplane parts and seaplane floats.

Various precautions were taken in the town in case of bombardment from the air and from the sea, but in the event the town was quiet. The closest Ventnor came to such eventualities was when H.M. Airship 'Beta' came within two miles of the pier in 1915 and when a Zeppelin had earlier passed over the town one night. Whereas at the start of the war there had been widespread fears of an invasion, it was soon clear that this was unlikely and some regular resort activities were quickly resumed. For instance, concerts were performed in the pier's Pavilion throughout the war years, including a string of visiting entertainers. By 1917, the most pressing issues had become the growing food shortages on the Island and the extensive damage done to sea walls and groynes after a severe storm hit Ventnor in November 1916.

Ventnor between the Wars

Like so many towns up and down the country, Ventnor lost many young men to the horrors of trench warfare in the Great War, their deaths commemorated on the War Memorial in Ventnor Park unveiled at a special ceremony in October 1920. However, as we have seen, the physical fabric of the town was little affected by the conflict and it was not long before summer holidaymakers at the very least began to return in the weeks of the ensuing seasons. Under the Railway Grouping Act of 1921, the train services into the town came under the control of the Southern Railway and the new company was not slow to stamp its corporate identity on the territory it served. The Isle of Wight was among its premier summer holiday destinations and was soon figuring in advertising copy, including national newspapers like The Times. In March 1923, Ventnor was singled out as a destination for Easter, vying with well-known mainland resorts like Torquay and Folkestone. On summer Saturdays, meanwhile, packed trains would pull into Ventnor from Ryde Pier Head station and hundreds of people would disgorge on to the platforms of the station off Mitchell Avenue and shortly get their first sight of the English Channel from the top of Grove Road, all of 280 feet above sea level. For the visitors with their suitcases and bags, often trailing fractious children, it was happily a downward walk to find the boarding houses where they were to make their weeklong stay. The better-off visitors, of course, either used the popular Brown's Station Bus or hired taxis from the standing rank at the station, to be taken to the many hotels that occupied prime sites in the resort, and not just in Ventnor but in Bonchurch and St. Lawrence, too. One young lad recalled life in a boarding house on Southgrove Terrace run by his parents in the later 1930s. It was always exciting to discover who was going to be staying in the house during the next week or fortnight. Each morning at breakfast time, a man from one of the local coach companies would call at boarding houses and take bookings for the trips that were organized for that day. Among them, Crinage's smart brown and cream vehicles offered daily excursions to Osborne, Blackgang, Bembridge and the Needles, all-day tours round the Island, along with afternoon and evening 'mystery tours'. The firm operated from the garage opposite the Post Office in Church Street.

One of the splendid charabancs that plied from Ventnor in the 1920s and early 1930s

For young children, of course, it was more likely that they would spend the day on the beach, while for the adults who did not favour a coach excursion, there were walks to be had. Most visitors went over the downs to Shanklin at some point in their stay, or else wandered through the Landslip to Luccombe for tea at the refreshment hut there. Down on the Esplanade, the children had the benefit of a new canoe lake, built by the District Council in 1935. There was roller skating on the pier and in Ventnor Pavilion on the Esplanade. By the summer season of 1938, a new cinema had also been opened in the town, with 'Oh Mr. Porter' among its first films. The 750-seat, brick-built 'Rex' was located at the eastern end of Belgrave Road on the site now occupied by the striking art deco style building, Kingsview. Otherwise, there was the beach itself to enjoy, whether swimming in the sea, sunbathing, or walking the Esplanade. There were rowing boats for hire, with or without a boatman, and motor launches that took visitors for trips out in the bay. A fleet of paddle steamers from the mainland made regular calls at the pier. Further out in the English Channel, transatlantic liners passed by at frequent intervals and it was a point of honour among local boys to be able to tell visitors the name of every one that went past. Finally, if you were holidaying in August, there was a chance that your stay might coincide with the annual Regatta or the annual Carnival. As well as the regular procession of floats, this typically involved a grand fair in Ventnor Park, with brass bands and dancing on the lawns, together with a Grand Fancy Dress Ball in the Town Hall. And the chances that you would enjoy such festivities in good weather were quite high, for Ventnor held the official sunshine record for the United Kingdom in seven out of the eleven years from 1927 to 1937.

A happy group on Ventnor beach, circa 1930. The bathing huts remain in use today.

The inter-war years, however, were not prosperous ones for Ventnor's existence as a leading resort for visitors in search of winter health, particularly those from the European continent. Many of its wealthier clientèle had failed to return after the war and so one of the fundamental bases of its all-year-round prosperity was much diminished. This was undoubtedly a reason why the *Royal Marine Hotel* closed its doors and was put up for sale in 1937. Despite this, Ventnor in the 1930s remained in large part very much the Victorian resort of the 1890s. There had been little twentieth-century building in the town, for the simple reason that there were very few sites left on which to build. Ribbons of new development stretched in places along Gills Cliff, the Whitwell Road and along Leeson Road. The overspill settlement of Upper Ventnor, just across the brow of the downs, had continued to grow. But otherwise, the picture of Ventnor as an Italian-looking resort clinging precariously to a succession of steep terraces above the sea remained as true for the 1930s as it had been fifty years before. However, in August 1936, a new building was opened in the resort that, in some more traditional eyes, deeply compromised the picturesque quality of the town. On the cliff-top site east of the Cascade, where the large stone Parsonage had stood in spacious gardens for almost a century, there had arisen a striking modern building, the Winter Gardens pavilion. Constructed of steel and concrete, it was *art deco* in style with a prominent glass-fronted staircase tower. Against the vertical lines of Ventnor's Victorian architecture, the building's emphasis on the horizontal was quite a shock to the eye, the windows of its café and solarium extending continuously across almost the entire width of the structure. Ventnor's sudden lurch into twentieth-century design had been heralded in many other resorts up and down Britain. The building has since most often been compared with the famous De La Warr Pavilion at Bexhill. It does not have anything like the same architectural 'panache' as Bexhill, but the Ventnor pavilion has by far the more stunning site. Facing south-west, it has spectacular views across the bay and out to sea. From its wide sun terraces, visitors can see the curvature of the earth on a clear day, so wide is the expanse of the horizon.

The Winter Gardens pavilion, shortly after completion. For a few observers, its brash modernism, including the use of concrete and steel, was an unsettling contrast alongside the more traditional structures above it.

Ventnor Urban District Council had purchased the Parsonage in 1929 and immediately began a programme of refurbishment for public use. The ground floor rooms were made over for reading, games and music, the upper floors as a refreshment area. The building re-opened as the 'Winter Gardens' in December of that year, the name chosen after a competition among townspeople. Some three years later, a scheme to turn the Parsonage into council offices met with strong protests in the town. It was then that the idea of a stylish new pavilion was floated. One councillor saw this as a vital opportunity for bringing renewed prosperity to Ventnor, but he also registered the necessity of ensuring that the town commissioned the right kind of building, both as to appearance and to its suitability.

The Council chose Mr. A. Douglas Clare, designer of the Sandown pavilion, as its architect and work proceeded rapidly over an eight-month period in 1936. At the heart of the building was a grand concert hall, designed to accommodate over 600 people. Its walls decorated in shades of mauve and green with bars of gold running round, with stage curtains in a silver and gold fabric, it formed a classic piece of *art deco* design. The concert hall was opened by August 1936, although the building as a whole was not finished until 1937. Thereafter the pavilion was quickly put into use. Aside from shows and concert performances, it hosted supper and tea dances, whist drives and all manner of competitions. There was also a resident orchestra and an entertainments manager. Even so, and despite the apparent popularity of the venue, the Winter Gardens registered an operating loss in 1937, much to the dismay of the local council. Seventy years on, that has unhappily been a very common story throughout the Pavilion's life. Today, like many similar seaside venues of the 1930s era, it increasingly shows signs of decay, large cracks showing in its external render and some of the *art deco* interior in need of renewal. Nothing, though, can detract from its superlative site, its bar and restaurant looking out directly across a vast expanse of the English Channel. It thus survives today as an intriguingly different edifice within what is otherwise a determinedly Victorian resort complex.

World War II

Anyone who has seen the film 'The Battle of Britain' (1969), with Laurence Olivier playing the role of Air Chief Marshal Dowding, may well remember the German aerial bombardment on Ventnor radar very early in the campaign. The film portrayed the real life attack that took place on 12th August 1940. The station's plotters (members of the WAAF) had observed a large force of some 200 aircraft over the Cherbourg peninsula that morning, heading north. As the formation of enemy aircraft approached Spithead, a detachment broke away and flew across the Island to Ventnor's radar installation on St. Boniface Down. Eighteen aircraft were involved in the attack. Four high-explosive bombs were dropped on the site, along with many delayed-action bombs. There was also extensive machine-gun fire. Miraculously, no lives were lost on the ground, but the radar facility sustained extensive damage and was forced to operate at reduced efficiency. On the 16th August, there was a second aerial bombardment of the station, this time involving the dropping of seven high-explosive bombs, together with more delayed-action bombs. Again, extensive damage was done to the facility, putting it 'off-air' for some time. It was a week before a reserve radar facility at Bembridge could be commissioned and the gap in the radar front line filled. The Ventnor station was not brought fully back into commission until the end of November.

High pylons had started appearing on the down above Ventnor late in 1938 and became a subject of much comment among the town's residents and visitors alike. There were initially four steel pylons of 350 feet in height, and four wooden pylons or towers of 240 feet, although it was soon established that one of the steel pylons was surplus to requirements and it was removed to Scotland. The steel pylons were for the transmitter aerials, the wooden ones for the receivers. A cluster of wooden huts housed the equipment and provided staff accommodation. After the bombing raids of August 1940, the equipment was placed in protected buildings and the WAAF operators were housed at a site in Down Lane and in requisitioned buildings in St. Boniface Road.

Ventnor radar pylons high on St.Boniface Down in 1940

The attacks on the radar station had impacts on the town itself. The blasts caused much damage to windows, including those of Holy Trinity Church. But there were also a number of stray bombs that damaged buildings, as well as others that were unexploded. Then, on August 19th 1940, the town itself became a direct bombing target. The attack came as a severe shock to its inhabitants, for there had been no air-raid warning. A bungalow in Zig-Zag road was wrecked and Belgrave Road was blocked by a huge crater, with associated damage to nearby buildings. The day after, August 20th, an unexploded device on Alpine Road detonated and caused yet further damage. These kinds of attacks became a pattern that was to continue intermittently for much of the duration of the war. Whilst elsewhere on the Island and on the mainland targets of Portsmouth and Southampton, night bombing raids became the norm, Ventnor remained largely a victim of the daylight raid, and particularly of the 'hit-and-run' variety. The aircraft usually came in pairs and flew in at exceptionally low altitudes in order to avoid being picked up by radar. On 18th August 1942, for instance, around teatime, two enemy Focke Wolfe Fw 190s suddenly swooped very low on the High Street, their bombs destroying an entire row of cottages and part of the police station. Many nearby buildings suffered collateral damage. On September 2nd, there was an almost identical raid that flattened a row of houses in North Street and a number of shops in the High Street. As before, other buildings suffered serious blast damage, including the Congregational Church. Most of these 'hit-and-run' raids were accompanied by intense machine-gun and cannon fire either before or after the bombs were released. One eye-witness described how the raids typically lasted no more than 5 minutes. The aircraft vanished into the sky almost as soon as they had appeared.

Over the entire course of the war, the Ventnor Urban District had 120 buildings damaged beyond repair and almost 1,500 needing attention as a result of the German bombing raids. Sixteen men and women were killed and many more were injured, some seriously. The last incident was when a V1 flying bomb came down on the golf course in Upper Ventnor on 14th July 1944.

The radar pylons and the damaged and destroyed town buildings were far from the only signs of Ventnor at war. As mentioned earlier, a section of Ventnor's pier neck, amounting to some 100 feet, was removed and dumped in the sea in 1940 in order to frustrate its use by any German invasion force. At the same time, the beach was closed to the population and subsequently festooned with steel scaffolding as a defence against tank landings. Large concrete blocks were then placed across the hair-pin roads leading up from the Esplanade, again in order to slow the progress of invasion forces. For Ventnor's schoolchildren, the war had meant evacuation to less risky locations nearby. For the town's hotels and boarding establishments, there were no longer any conventional visitors, merely squads of servicemen and other wartime personnel to be billeted. The war's overall impact on the town was far greater than anything the town experienced between 1914 and 1918. And recovery was quite slow under the shadow of post-war shortage and austerity. Along Belgrave Road, one of the town's prime resort sites, only gaping spaces marked the position of the *Royal Marine Hotel*, while some of the High Street had vanished too.

Twilight and rebirth

By the 1930s, Ventnor's prosperity had become very firmly anchored to its summer holiday trades. There were still some out-of-season visitors, but the winter patronage that had been so important a part of its Victorian prosperity had faded very significantly by that time. With the coming of peace in Europe in the early summer of 1945, the summer trade began to recover and, by the late 1940s and early 1950s, had attained the condition of a post-war boom. Record numbers of passengers were being carried in the high season by the Portsmouth-Ryde ferries and the Island railways found their resources stretched to the limit, especially along the Ryde-Ventnor route. Weekday timetables had three trains per hour between Ryde and Ventnor. On summer Saturdays, there were two per hour to Ventnor and one each per hour to Sandown and Shanklin. Over the whole of a summer Saturday, no less than 46 trains made the trip from Ryde to Ventnor, each carrying some 450 passengers or more. In other words, 20,000 or more tourists could pass through Ventnor's main railway terminus on a busy August Saturday or on a summer Bank Holiday. Many of them were day-trippers, of course, as were the similar crowds that arrived by road coaches or disembarked from steamers docking at the pier after its full re-opening in the 1955 season. But a proportion of rail passengers still came as weekly visitors, providing vital income for the ranks of boarding houses that dominated Ventnor's ascending terraces. The town's attractive annual guide-books of the period paint a picture of a resort that was on a tide of renewed prosperity, with a wide range of entertainments to occupy visitors, not forgetting the beach and the sea where, on hot days, it was almost standing room only judging from photographs taken at the time. You could barely see the beach for sunbathers and deck-chairs. At the Winter Gardens, Islanders would often join the ranks of summer visitors to dance to Victor Silvester, Terry Lightfoot and other big bands of the day. For the young, there were dodgem cars and other amusements in the former Ventnor Pavilion. The town also hosted 'Old Folks Weeks', providing welcome holidays for pensioners from all over the country.

Ventnor Station in December 1963, with a train about to depart for Ryde Pier Head

Unhappily, the early post-war prosperity proved something of a swan-song. By the 1960s, the cheap overseas package holiday was beginning to make inroads into the traditional English seaside holiday. At the same time, the steady rise in car ownership saw the pattern of mass day trips by public transport slowly but inexorably fade. Nationalisation of the railways in 1948 also brought another spectre on to the horizon: the future survival of the Island railways. The line from Merstone to Ventnor West was the first casualty, closing to all traffic in September 1952. It had had a life of little more than fifty years, but it had been running an operating loss since before the war. Located almost a mile west of the main town, it had always been something of a luxury, for all its spectacular scenic attractions. But this was not the case with the main station at the top of Grove Road. In fact, under the infamous Beeching Plan of 1963, *all* the Island lines were earmarked for closure. The news came as a profound shock to Islanders and to businesses, although closure had been contemplated by railway managers some ten years before. The news gave rise to one of the most contested and heated disputes that the Island had ever had with central government. The eventual upshot was that it was agreed to retain the line from Ryde Pier to Shanklin, but all other railway services were to be withdrawn, including that from Shanklin to Ventnor. Huge local political efforts were directed towards attempts to retain the route through to Ventnor, but they ultimately fell victim to political expediency at ministerial level. Although there was twice as much passenger traffic to Sandown and to Shanklin as there was to Ventnor, there was common consent that retention of the line to Ventnor, along with its electrification, could have been achieved without operating at a loss. A mass meeting in Ventnor's Town Hall in March 1966, just a month before withdrawal of the train service, was attended by over 500 of the town's residents. The cost of upgrading the line between Shanklin and Ventnor was known to be of the order of £100,000.

And given that the town accounted for nearly one third of the Ryde-Ventnor line's income, it was seen as a fair investment.

It was not to be, however. The Ventnor line closed to all traffic on 18th April 1966. By the end of that summer season, the effects on the town's summer tourist traffic were already clear. Holiday bookings were down by about 25 per cent and casual day traffic had fallen much more. British Railways had expected that travellers wanting to visit Ventnor would in future travel by rail to Shanklin and then transfer to buses. A replacement bus service was inaugurated from Shanklin station for the purpose. However, in the event, most visitors chose to travel to Ventnor all the way by bus from Ryde, so denting most of the traffic and income forecasts on which the retained section of railway between Ryde and Shanklin had been justified. It was a spectacular error of judgement on the part of railway decision-makers. Between 1965 and 1967, passenger numbers booked through to Ventnor by train from the mainland had dropped by 80,000. By 1983, the bus link from Shanklin station to Ventnor had to be abandoned for want of custom and it was not until 2004 that the present 'Ventnor Rail Link' service was introduced.

Ventnor did not give up its struggle for the railway to be retained. Various groups, including the County Council and the Town Council, repeatedly sought to bring pressure for closure to be reversed and the railway authorities appeared to remain open to persuasion. Much of the track remained in place until 1970, for instance, so that re-opening remained a practical option. However, the County Council refused to provide any financial contribution to the line's reinstatement and the campaign finally collapsed. It was a decision that was to mark the beginning of a pattern of investment by the County Council and by South Wight Borough Council in which Ventnor was repeatedly marginalized over subsequent years. The Ventnor Railway Association was formed in the early 1990s as a lobby group to try to bring about re-instatement of the line. The new Isle of Wight Council also commissioned a report early in the new millennium that recommended re-instatement, but dependent on money from central government. The long tunnel under St. Boniface Down remains in fair condition, so that re-opening is not wholly far-fetched. However, the railway privatization of the 1990s has not really been a success as far as the remaining Ryde-Shanklin route goes. Despite quite heavy passenger loadings, it requires a proportionately vast level of subsidy under the financial structures that current railway operation in Britain involves.

The other major sources of summer visitors to the town, the road coaches and the steamer excursions, also increasingly dried up after the later 1960s. Rising car ownership took its toll on Island coach firms. Where once it was not uncommon for Ventnor to see forty or more coaches in the town at lunchtime of a summer season, by the 1970s this traffic was seriously in decline. Equally, and as described earlier, the pier's landing stages were taken out of commission as their condition deteriorated and, eventually, landing was no longer possible at all. The pier itself was subsequently condemned and dismantled. The loss of both railway station and pier, in particular, removed two of Ventnor's vital arteries. The town entered the twilight era that characterized so many English seaside places in the last decades of the twentieth century: crumbling public facilities, boarded up shops, faded lodging houses and hotels, not to mention unemployment which hit new peaks on the Island in the mid-1980s. Moreover, what post-war developments there were tended to dilute and, in a few cases destroy, the town's unique Victorian ambience. The Island's town planners of the 1960s and 1970s seemed to think that thrusting, amorphous-looking blocks of flats were an appropriate accompaniment to Victorian eclecticism. Many of the town's boarding houses were subdivided (sometimes quite insensitively) into flats as their original purpose became redundant. Recently, one resident recalled his teenage years in Ventnor in the 1980s as a time when you tended not to mention that you came from the town. It had a run-down character, apparently quite out of kilter with the modern age. There were other developments, too, that seemed to compound the problem over the years. Serious land movement in Bath Road in 1960 had resulted in the need to demolish the *Balmoral Hotel*, a prominent Victorian structure at the western end of the Esplanade. *Steephill Castle*, a jewel of the picturesque movement of the 1830s, was finally demolished in 1964 and the estate land used for housing. A string of fires also caused extensive damage to buildings and resulted in further demolitions. Among the victims were the *Beach Hotel* on the Esplanade and the *Rex* cinema. Both had been derelict for some years, much to the dismay of local hoteliers who repeatedly had to petition South Wight Borough Council for it to become more active in supporting tourism in the town. Even today, in 2010, there is an old Victorian building in a tumbledown state in a prime site on the Esplanade.

Not surprisingly perhaps, there were a few who sought to take Ventnor forward by floating a series of 'grand projects'. A multi-million pound marina was one of the more outlandish. Its proposers, the Ventnor Harbour Company, envisaged a passenger ferry terminal, berthing for over 500 yachts, some 400 residential units, not to mention 100 holiday apartments and a host of shops and restaurants. A tram service was intended to link the various parts of the development and parking was to be provided for 1500 cars. An earlier idea, known as 'The Cascades Project', envisaged a leisure complex on the Eastern Esplanade, an escalator in a translucent tube linking the Esplanade to the Winter Gardens, a cable car from the Pierhead to the Winter Gardens, renovation of the Winter Gardens as a multi-purpose sports hall, health and theatre complex, and the formation of a special botanical enclosure with exotic plants and butterflies. The naturalist David Bellamy lent his name to the latter idea. As one might well have anticipated, none of the investment capital for any of these schemes materialized. What happened instead was that there was a slow realization that Ventnor already had a 'brand' that could be redeveloped and marketed for the turn of the millennium. Victorian architecture had been undergoing a steady re-assessment since John Betjeman and others had succeeded in preventing the destruction of London's St. Pancras station and other major buildings like it. By the 1990s, this preservationist movement had extended to seaside towns. A Civic Trust was thus established to aid the town's regeneration. English Heritage gave the green light to a Conservation Area Partnership Scheme. A new seafront pumping station for the town's waste water was completed alongside the new Ventnor Haven, the station building topped by a Victorian style rotunda that afforded new viewpoints of sea and shore. On an area of the Esplanade directly beneath the Winter Gardens, a large boat-building shed has recently been erected, together with a bar-restaurant. Within the newly-built Haven, meanwhile, a fishing jetty has been added with fish-processing sheds and fishmonger's shop. Local fishermen not only ply the general public with their catches, as they did more than 150 years ago, but supply many local restaurants and businesses too. Weather and tide permitting, there are now power boat trips along the Undercliff coast, as well as boats available for fishing expeditions. Further west, at the Botanic Gardens, a new multi-million pound visitor centre opened in May 2000, helping to consolidate the Gardens as one of the Island's premier visitor attractions.

Ultimately, though, the key to Ventnor's revival in the new millennium has been the property price boom and the emergence of Ventnor as an attractive site for second homes. Its relative isolation from the rest of the island, its spectacular terraced site and its surviving period charm has proved to be an irresistible formula. The price of nineteenth-century villas multiplied three and four-fold over a period of less than a decade. At the same time, former public buildings, hotels and lodging houses have been steadily redeveloped.

The art deco style 'Kingsview' building, constructed on the site of the old Rex Cinema

The site of the *Rex* cinema, following the entire structure's gutting by fire in 1993, became home to an award-winning, art deco style apartment building that makes inspired use of its corner clifftop site. The former *King Charles Hotel*, at the junction of Grove Road and Spring Hill, has been transformed into apartments (King Charles Court) without in any way compromising any of its classical Italianate frontage. On the Esplanade, meanwhile, the old *Metropole Hotel* had become unsafe and was demolished to be replaced by *The Metropole*, a five to six storey structure with commercial units on the ground floor and apartments above. Opinion remains divided as to how far the design pays service to the Victorian hotel that it replaced. However, the commercial facilities have proved resoundingly popular among residents and visitors, and not just in the high season. Under the shelter of its long verandah, visitors can enjoy flavours of Mediterranean living, all within a stone's throw of sand and sea. Further along the Esplanade, several former hotels and boarding houses have been re-cast to accommodate new restaurants. Higher up, on Hambrough Road, a large cliff-top boarding house has become the *Hambrough Hotel*, its restaurant granted a Michelin star in early 2009. Westward along Belgrave Road, beyond the former site of Ventnor's *Royal Marine Hotel*, the *Wellington Hotel* and the *Royal Hotel* both continue the traditions of accommodation and fare that characterized Ventnor in its prime.

The Royal Hotel on Belgrave Road, well sheltered from prevailing winds and set in fabulous garden grounds. Founded in 1830 as Fisher's Hotel, it has undergone a succession of enlargements in the intervening 180 years.

Finally, if one negotiates the precipitous hair-pin bends of Bath Road back down to the Western Esplanade, there is Ventnor's *Spyglass Inn*, located on a rock promontory. The inn was previously *Undercliff House* and the building originally started life as a bath house for the Royal Hotel. On windy days, the waves pound and reverberate on the rocks below. Inside the Inn, walls are festooned with old nautical paraphernalia, a timely reminder of how Ventnor's earliest inhabitants won their living from sea and shore.

The Spyglass Inn, formerly Undercliff House, overlooking the English Channel at the western end of the Esplanade. The building was once a bath house for the Royal Hotel, hence the name of Bath Road.

In the town centre itself, in and around the High Street, evidence of Ventnor's revival is less, but the signs are there even so. Several new retail businesses have appeared in the last few years. A number of new cafés have quickly attracted custom from residents and visitors alike and in all seasons. There are also several new bars and restaurants. It is true that there are still empty shops, but there are enough genuine antique and curio establishments (including charity shops) to give parts of the High Street a flavour of the Portobello Road, places for visitors to browse and strike a bargain and, by most reckonings, infinitely preferable to the more common souvenir shops that dominate many seaside towns.

By 2009, of course, Ventnor, like every town and city in the country at large, was suffering under the 'credit crunch'. The resort's booming property market was first of all 'flat-lining' and, later, in retreat. For all the attractions of the Undercliff, taking in Bonchurch and St. Lawrence alongside Ventnor, the effect has been widespread, with ranks of unsold properties on agents' books. However, there has been no fundamental downturn in visitors. Out-of-season trade has also held up, providing continual reminders of the reasons why the town became such a favoured winter retreat in the Victorian age. There are also further grounds for optimism. Ventnor has a powerful sense of community and never more so than in difficult times. Its annual Carnival continues to offer a remarkable piece of social theatre, a powerful evocation of community spirit and involvement. Ventnor has long been a magnet for Jazz enthusiasts, with outdoor as well as indoor billings throughout the main season. Ventnor's Heritage Museum has steadily built its reputation as custodian of the town's historic and cultural identity, its monthly lectures typically packed to the door. The Undercliff remains a highly attractive place for retirement, or, as one journalist recently put it, a retreat for retired colonels and amateur botanists, a hideaway for middle-class escapees from the mainland. Charles Dickens, along with a host of other Victorian writers and artists, began the tendency more than 150 years ago, of course. For some, Ventnor and the Undercliff appear unambiguously a world apart, a feature that the drama of the approaches to it plainly underline. And on a late November day, when even the Island's capital, Newport, is clouded and cool, the balm of Ventnor's terraces can feel like a foreign clime, as if a part of the Island has temporarily drifted off to a sub-tropical sea. Flowers bloom wild on rocky banks. Succulents tumble over walls, their occasional pink and purple rosettes a tantalizing hint of another world. You may even be lucky enough to spot one of Ventnor's green wall lizards, introduced, as you may have guessed, by a Victorian naturalist. It does not take long to appreciate why the Undercliff was such a favoured spot for Victorian consumptives. And it is not hard to see why some leading newspaper journalists now talk of Victoria's 'Garden Isle' as well on the way to re-inventing itself, with Ventnor arguably at its apex, recalling the era when it was labelled 'Queen' of the Undercliff.

The Western Cliffs and Ventnor Bay, viewed from the Winter Gardens. The new Victorian style rotunda hides a waste pumping station.

Ventnor Botanic Gardens: part of the Mediterranean Terrace in June

Ventnor circa 1920

The map opposite depicts Ventnor around 1920, taken from one of the Isle of Wight guide-books of the time. Apart from suburban housing infill to the west of the town and also in Upper Ventnor, the street plan remains much the same today. The map shows the site of the Royal Victoria Pier, the site of Steephill Castle, as well as the locations of the town's two railway stations. On the shoreline east of Ventnor Bay, new sea defences have created a continuous promenade to Bonchurch. A similar promenade extends across Castle Cove (below the site of the old castle) towards Steephill Cove.

The map is intended primarily as an aid to the text and should not be relied upon as a modern guide. Modern maps are obtainable from local newsagents and bookstores. A basic map of the town and its environs is also produced by the Ventnor Business Association, available free from a number of outlets in the town.

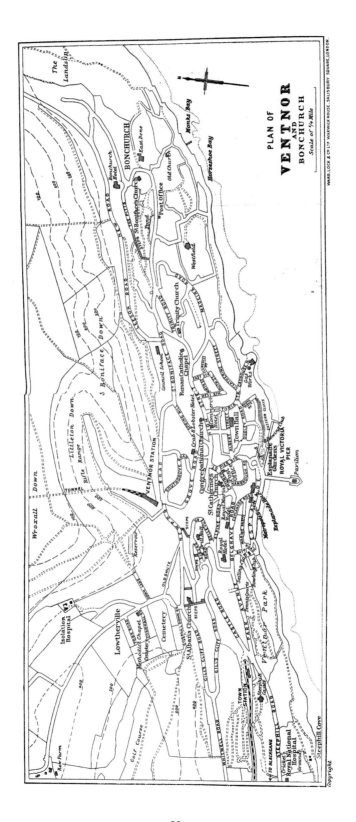

PLAN OF
VENTNOR
AND
BONCHURCH

Scale of ⅛ Mile

WARD, LOCK & Cº Lᵈ WARWICK HOUSE, SALISBURY SQUARE, LONDON.

53

Walks

Local newsagents and bookshops stock a good range of walking guides and these notes are not intended to replace them. The Museum and the Town Council also publish guides of their own, known as 'Town Trails'. However, it was thought that it might be helpful to readers to offer advice on walks that would illuminate some of the features described in this book. As this is a landslip zone, great care should be taken to observe all notices erected by the Isle of Wight Council regarding the dangers of walking along cliff and coastal paths.

*The Western Cliffs that feature in **Walk III**. The white obelisk that is just visible to the left centre of the picture marks the eastern edge of Steephill Cove*

I.   The easiest of routes (in that it is all on the level) begins at the *Spyglass Inn* and, working eastward, takes in the length of the Esplanade, the Haven area, and then the long stretch of sea wall that finishes at Bonchurch Shore, a walking time of around 30 minutes. At the bottom of Shore Road, a blue plaque records how Bonchurch was a favourite haunt of writers and artists in the nineteenth century. The return leg can be back the same way, but the more energetic may take the road up from the Shore to Bonchurch village road with its picturesque pond and its café. It is then only a short walk westward past Holy Trinity Church to the upper end of Ventnor High Street. Continuing down the High Street, past its lines of shops, eventually brings up the traffic lights at the junction with Pier Street. Turning left down Pier Street, it is then an easy if steep descent back down to the Esplanade, total walking time in this case around 50 minutes.

II. Another fairly easy route follows the line of one of Ventnor's rock terraces. Beginning outside the Post Office in Church Street, just west of the Pier Street traffic lights, it proceeds westward into Belgrave Road, historically one of the most favoured spots in the town, and still the location of several premier hotels. The end of Belgrave Road leads into Park Avenue, with its pleasure gardens on the south side and its stone villas on the north. At the western end of Park Avenue, a blue plaque on the stone wall on the north side of the road recalls the former site of Steephill Castle. Continuing west along Steephill Road for about a third of a mile leads to the site of the former National Chest Hospital, now Ventnor Botanic Gardens. The walk takes about 20 minutes. The return leg can be back the same way. Alternatively, the more energetic may take the coast path that can be accessed at the south-east corner of the Botanic Gardens. This route is described in Walk **III**, but in the reverse direction.

III. This walk takes the coast path and involves steep gradients and steps. It begins in the car park on the Western Cliffs, accessed from Bath Road. The initial route is westward across gently rising meadows, but this gives way to a long flight of downward steps and then a steady ascent to a promontory above Castle Cove. In places the coast path has had to be re-routed due to landslips, so it is important to follow the signage with care. Descending to Castle Cove, the walk then takes in the sea wall round to Steephill Cove with its cluster of fishermen's cottages and holiday homes. This is another 20-minute walk, slightly longer if paced for the less agile of foot. The return can be back the same way. Alternatively, a steep narrow path adjacent to the seaside café leads up to the south-east corner of the Botanic Gardens. From the Gardens car park, there is then easy access to the main road back into Ventnor, via Steephill Road, Park Avenue and Belgrave Road.

IV. The most demanding of the walks listed here is the one that leads from the High Street into the lower half of Spring Hill and then turns sharp left outside the Heritage Museum into Grove Road. There follows an increasingly steep ascent to Mitchell Avenue, close to 300 feet above sea level. In the process, walkers will gain good sight of the former St. Catherine's Home, as well as some of Ventnor's surviving Regency buildings, not to mention excellent views out to sea. This walk is also memorable in that it is the one that summer holidaymakers travelling by train often had to tackle, laden with their suitcases, when it was time to return home. At various intervals along the way, seats are still to be found from that era where weary legs and fractious children would pause for rest. The entrance to the old railway station lies immediately across from Mitchell Avenue, the entire station site now occupied by light industry. However, at the extreme right just inside the entrance road there is a marked path that leads up on to St. Boniface Down, a walk that extends up almost to the 800-foot contour. On a clear day, the rewarding views are breathtaking, but it is not a climb for the unfit or the infirm. In poor weather, moreover, the Down often disappears in cloud and so extra care is needed. Allow 50 minutes at least for the ascent from High Street via Grove Road to the top of the down. The return can obviously be made more quickly, but the descent immediately above the old station site can be very slippery in wet conditions.

Ventnor Botanic Gardens: the sub-tropical palm garden

Acknowledgements

The author records very generous thanks to leading local historian, Fay Brown, for making so many of her personal research files available in the writing of this book. Much material has also been gleaned from the extensive holdings at Ventnor Heritage Museum and many thanks are due to its Curator, Graham Bennett, for providing such a welcome environment for research. The original idea for the booklet was Graham's, and both he and Fay have repeatedly given of their time in combing early drafts for inaccuracies and omissions, as well as providing suggestions for improvement. I am also indebted to Alan and Sharon Champion, Roger Silsbury, Michael and Violetta Vokes, and Nigel Traylen for looking over the draft text. The illustrations are drawn from the Museums's holdings, from the extensive collection belonging to Fay Brown, and from the author. If there any instances where it is thought that copyright has been infringed, the Museum would be grateful to receive details.

Bibliography

The following includes a list of some of the principal published materials used in writing this book, as well as suggestions for further reading:

Black, A. & C. *Black's Picturesque Guide to the Isle of Wight* (Adam and Charles Black, 7th ed., 1878)

Brannon, G. *Picture of the Isle of Wight* (Wootton , c. 1841)

Bray, P. *Railways into Ventnor* (Ventnor and District Local History Society, n.d.)

Bray, P. *Radar at Ventnor, 1939-1945* (Ventnor and District Local History Society, n.d.)

Bray, P and Brown, F., *The Ventnor Area at War, 1939-1945* (Ventnor & District Local History Society, n.d.)

Brinton, R. *Victorian Island: the Isle of Wight in Victorian photographs* (Dovecote Press, 1994)

Brown, F.H. *A Tale of Two Buildings: the Ventnor and Bonchurch Literary and Scientific Institution and the Town Hall* (Ventnor and District Local History Society, n.d.)

Chambers, V. (ed.) *Old Men Remember: Life on Victoria's Island* (Ventnor and District Local History Society, 1988)

Champion, A. *Vectis: a bibliographical catalogue of Isle of Wight books* (5 vols., Alan Champion, 1997-1999) – see also *www.iwhistory.com*

Clark, J. *The Influence of Climate in the Prevention and Cure of Chronic Disease* (John Murray, 2nd ed., 1830

Davenport Adams, W.H., *The Isle of Wight: its history, topography and antiquities* (T. Nelson and Sons, 1882)

Freeman, M. *A Winter Sanatorium: Ventnor as a health resort in the Victorian era* (Ventnor and District Local History Society, 2009)

Hyland, P. *Wight: Biography of an Island* (Gollancz, 1985)

Isle of Wight Mercury

Jenkinson, H. I. *Jenkinson's Smaller Practical Guide to the Isle of Wight* (2nd ed., Edward Stanford, 1879)

Knight, W. J. *Knight's Household Almanack and Ventnor and Bonchurch Yearbook* (W.J. Knight, 1889)

Knight, W. J., *The Ventnor Red Book* (18th issue, W.J. Knight, 1908)

Laidlaw, E. F. *The Story of the Royal National Hospital Ventnor* (E.F. Laidlaw, 1990)

McInnes, R. *The Isle of Wight Illustrated* (Robin McInnes, 1989)

McInnes, R. *The Garden Isle: Landscape Paintings of the Isle of Wight, 1790-1920* (Robin McInnes, 1990)

Martin, G. A. *The Undercliff of the Isle of Wight; its climate, history and natural productions* (John Churchill, 1849)

Mate, W. *Mate's Illustrated Ventnor* (4th ed., W. Mate & Sons, 1908)

Maycock, R. and Silsbury, R. *The Isle of Wight Railways from 1923 onwards* (Oakwood Press, 2006)

Mogridge, G. *Wanderings in the Isle of Wight* (The Religious Tract Society, 1846)

Murray, J.   *Murray's Handbook: Isle of Wight* (John Murray, 1898)

Nelson, T.   *Nelson's Pictorial Guide Books: the Isle of Wight: Part Fourth: Ventnor, the Undercliff and Back of the Island* (T. Nelson and Sons, 1869)

Parr, D.A.   *Ventnor and District: Britain in Old Photographs* (Sutton, 1996)

Paye, P. *The Ventnor West Branch* (Wild Swan Publications, 1992)

Payne, E.D.G.   *The Harbour and Piers of Ventnor, 1843-1988* (Ventnor and District Local History Society, n.d.)

The Times

Venables, E   *A Guide to the Undercliff* (Knight and Sons, c. 1867)

Ward, Lock & Co. *Pictorial and Descriptive Guide to the Isle of Wight* (21st ed., 1925-6)

Whitehead, J. L.   *The Climate of the Undercliff* (J. & A. Churchill, 1881)

Whitehead, J. L.   *The Undercliff of the Isle of Wight: past and present* (Knight's Library, 1911)

Williamson, J.M. *The Climate of the Undercliff* (Spottiswoode & Co. , 1877)

Wilson, L. *Portrait of the Isle of Wight* (Robert Hale, 1965)